chicken *perfection*

HINKLER
BOOKS

chicken
perfection

Food Editor
Ellen Argyriou

Creative Director
Sam Grimmer

Project Editor
Lara Morcombe

HINKLER
BOOKS

First published in 2004 by Hinkler Books Pty Ltd
17–23 Redwood Drive
Dingley, VIC 3172 Australia
www.hinklerbooks.com
Reprinted.2004

© Text and Design Hinkler Books Pty Ltd
© Step-by-Step Shots and Hero Shots on pages 47, Hinkler Books Pty Ltd
© Hero Shots on pages 12, 13, 14, 15, 16, 17, 18, 19, 20, 21, 24, 25, 26, 27, 28, 29,
30, 31, 34-35, 36-37, 38, 39, 40, 41, 42-43, 46, 48-49, 50, 51, 52-53, 54,
55, 56, 57, 60, 61, 62-63, 64-65, 66, 67, 68, 69, 70-71, 72, 73
R&R Publications licensed to Hinkler Books Pty Ltd

ISBN: 1 74121 825 X
EAN: 9 781741 218251

Printed and bound in China

contents

an introduction to chicken and poultry cooking

A Whole chicken, chicken cuts, ground chicken, stir-fry pieces, casserole pieces and even chicken bones to make stock are readily available in the market place, making chicken the number one home-cooked fast food.

From a quick stir-fry to a roasted chicken dinner or tasty casserole, chicken can be cooked and served in a great variety of ways.

nutritional value

• It's rich in protein containing all of the 8 essential amino acids.

• Vitamins are well represented, particularly vitamins A and B. Iron, phosphorus and zinc are also present.

• It's low in fat, particularly when the skin is removed.

• It's tender to eat and easy to digest making it especially suited for infants, children and the elderly.

purchasing and storage tips

fresh chicken

• Make it the last purchase on your shopping list. Place the chicken in an insulated bag to keep it cold on the way home.

• Refrigerate the chicken immediately after you arrive home. Remove it from the package, rinse and pat dry. Place in a dish and cover loosely with plastic wrap. Place in the coldest part of the refrigerator, below 4°C (39°F). It may be kept for 3 days. Treat chicken pieces in the same way.

• If chicken needs to be stored longer, it is better to buy ready frozen chicken than to buy fresh and freeze at home.

• If the chicken pieces are to be purchased and frozen for future use, make sure they are fresh and not previously frozen. Wipe dry with paper towel then pack flat in plastic freezer bags. Extract air by pushing out towards the opening, and tape the bag closed. Label and date packages.

frozen chicken

• Make sure the chicken is frozen solid and that there are no signs of a torn package and no ice deposits in the bottom of the package. This is a sign of partial thaw and refreezing which may result in a higher bacterial count in the chicken.

• Place in the freezer immediately on arrival home.

• Thaw frozen chicken thoroughly before cooking to avoid toughening the texture

and to reduce the chance of some parts being undercooked. Under-cooked parts could harbor food-spoiling bacteria.

- Do not refreeze thawed chicken. It is advisable to cook the thawed chicken and freeze it when cooked if necessary.

- To thaw a frozen chicken, remove it from the wrap and place it on a rack in a dish to allow liquid to collect beneath the chicken. Cover loosely with plastic wrap and place in the refrigerator for 24 hours. This is the safest way to thaw. Thawing on the kitchen counter must be avoided for bacterial growth may commence on the top area first thawed. Thawing in the microwave is quick and safe, but remember to follow the manufacturer's instructions.

preparation for cooking

whole chickens for roasting

Scrape inside the cavity with a fork to release the remaining giblets. Rinse under running water inside and out. Pat dry inside and out with paper towels. You may rub the chicken inside and out with half a lemon, squeezing out juice as you rub. It gives the chicken a delightful fresh flavor.

to truss a chicken

Cut a piece of kitchen string long enough to encircle the chicken twice. Pin back the wings and insert a skewer through the body under the legs and through to the other side. Pick up the string at its center and loop around the pope's nose (rump). Holding the string in each hand loop around the drumstick ends then cross over pulling the legs together. Loop around the skewer at each side, then take the string along the sides and loop around the wings. Turn the chicken over and tie. Trussing keeps the chicken in shape while roasting.

for small chickens: Loop string around pope's nose, cross over then loop around each drumstick and pull together and tie.

chicken breast fillets

pan-fried breast fillets: It is best to have an even thickness to ensure even contact with the bottom of the hot pan. Place the fillet between 2 sheets of plastic wrap and pound the higher center lightly with the side of a meat mallet or a rolling pin until the thickness evens out.

chicken schnitzel

A thinner fillet is needed. Pound as above but with outward strokes to extend the fillet outwards making it thinner.

thigh fillets

The bone and skin have been removed. These fillets may be used for pan frying, for schnitzels or pounded out very thinly and formed into rolls with stuffing.

It is best to slit the white membrane on the shiny side of the fillet in several places with a small pointed knife. This will allow the fillet to stretch and flatten as it is pounded. Proceed as for chicken fillets above.

chicken wings

Wings may be cooked whole or joints separated. For whole wings turn the wing tip behind the end joint to form an attractive triangular shape.

to make mini drumsticks

Use the first joint of the wing which has a meaty bulb at the end. Hold the end of the bone firmly; with a small sharp knife scrape the flesh around the bone towards and almost to the top end. Push the meat over the end to form a small drumstick. Marinate and broil for finger food.

handy cooking tips

1 To roast chicken with a crisp skin: Place the washed chicken in the refrigerator uncovered for 2 hours. The cold air dries the skin which when roasted becomes crisp and tasty.

2 Boneless chicken breast fillets are very tender and will toughen if overcooked. Cook for 3–4 minutes each side under a preheated broiler. Brushing with a little oil or a marinade before cooking will keep the fillets juicy and tender.

Thicker pieces of chicken such as half breast with bone and skin, Maryland pieces or drumsticks and thighs need lower heat and longer cooking time to allow the heat to penetrate into the center. Place the broiler tray in a lower position to be further away from the heat. Cook for 5–8 minutes each side or longer if very thick, then move the broiler tray closer to the heat to brown and crisp for final cooking. Pierce the chicken with a skewer, if juices run clear the chicken is ready. If they are a pink color more cooking is needed.

3 Barbecued chicken drumsticks are often served blackened on the outside and rare in the center. Never serve rare chicken as the bacteria that may be present will not have been destroyed. To cook correctly, place the chicken on the cooler part of the barbecue, or on a wire rack raised above the heat. Cook for 20–25 minutes turning occasionally to allow heat to penetrate to the center, then place directly onto the hot broiler bars for 5 minutes to brown and crisp, turning frequently.

4 Chicken pieces for cooking in a simmer sauce must be first browned all over to seal in the juices. Heat a little oil in a suitable saucepan and brown a few pieces at a time. Remove then add the next batch. If the pan is crowded the temperature will drop, juices will be extracted and browning prevented. Drain the fat from the pan before adding the simmer sauce. Bring quickly to the boil, turn down to a simmer and return the browned chicken to the pan. Simmer for 35–40 minutes to cook the chicken to the bone.

5 To poach chicken breasts for use in cold dishes, salads, and sandwich and focaccia fillings: Place chicken in a saucepan, add a piece of onion, celery, carrot, salt and a few peppercorns. Pour over enough hot water to almost cover and bring to a simmer, cover and simmer slowly for 20–25 minutes until tender. Allow to cool in the liquid; reserve the stock for other use. Whole fresh chicken may be poached in the same way for 30–35 minutes. When cool remove the skin and carefully ease the chicken flesh from the bones.

to joint a chicken

It is more economical to cut a whole chicken into pieces yourself than to buy ready cut pieces. Use a large sharp knife and a chopping board.

1 Place chicken on its back with legs towards you. Pull the left leg away from the body and cut through the skin to expose the joint. Bend the leg backwards at the joint to dislocate it. Cut through the joint to free the leg. Turn chicken around and remove the other leg. If you wish to separate the drumstick from the thigh locate the joint and cut through.

2 To remove the breast cut through the flap of skin on each side and continue to cut through the fine rib bones until you meet resistance from stronger bones. Gently chop through these bones to the neck on both sides and cut free of the backbone.

3 To divide the whole breast, place skin side down and press to open out wide. Lay the carving knife along the line of white cartilage, press down hard or hit the back of the knife with a meat mallet to insert it into the cartilage, then cut through to separate the 2 sides. The wings may be removed at the main joint next to the breast or cut off at the second joint. Each breast may be cut into 2 portions if desired.

starters
snacks
and
savories

chicken and prune roll

ingredients

2 bacon slices, finely chopped
1 medium onion, finely chopped
5 pitted prunes, chopped
500 g (1 lb) ground chicken
2 tablespoons dried breadcrumbs
$1/2$ teaspoon salt
$1/2$ teaspoon pepper
1 teaspoon cumin
1 egg, lightly beaten
1 sheet frozen puff pastry
5 pitted whole prunes
1 tablespoon milk
2 teaspoons poppy seeds

serves 6-8

1 In a small heated pan, place bacon and onions and cook while stirring for 1 minute. Mix the chopped prunes, chicken, breadcrumbs, salt, pepper, cumin, egg, and the bacon and onion mixture. Combine well.

preparation time
20 minutes

cooking time
40 minutes

nutritional value per serve
fat: 9.3 g
carbohydrate: 11.2 g
protein: 13.4 g

2 Preheat the oven to 200°C (400°F, gas mark 6). Line a baking sheet with baking paper and place thawed puff pastry onto the baking sheet. Spoon $1/2$ of the ground chicken mixture along the center of the sheet in an even strip about 3 inches wide and to the edge of the pastry at both ends. Arrange the 5 whole prunes along the center then cover with remaining ground chicken and smooth to even thickness.

3 Brush the back strip of pastry with water, lift the front pastry over the chicken and lift the back pastry to overlap the front. Press lightly along the seam to seal. Lift paper and turn the chicken roll over to rest on the seam join. Pull paper to bring it into the center of the tray, trim off paper overhang. Glaze roll with milk and sprinkle with poppy seeds.

4 Bake in the oven for 15 minutes. Turn oven down to 180°C (350°F, gas mark 4) and continue cooking for 25 minutes until golden. Slice and serve with salad garnish.

chicken yakitori

preparation time:
10 minutes, plus several hours or overnight marinating

cooking time
4-5 minutes

nutritional value per serve
fat: 5.3 g
carbohydrate: 15.8 g
protein: 15.2 g

ingredients

500 g (1 lb) chicken tenderloins
4 tablespoons teriyaki sauce
4 tablespoons honey
1 clove garlic, minced
¼ teaspoon ground ginger
4 bamboo skewers, soaked
oil for greasing
makes 15-20

1 In a non-metallic bowl, place chicken. In a separate bowl, combine teriyaki sauce, honey, garlic and ginger. Pour over chicken. Cover and place in refrigerator to marinate for several hours or overnight.

2 Thread 1 or 2 tenderloins onto each skewer, using weaving motion. Heat barbeque or electric broiler to medium-high. Grease broiler bars lightly with oil.

3 Place skewers in a row and cook for 2 minutes on each side, brushing with marinade as they cook and when turned. Remove to a large plate. Serve immediately as finger food.

and cooked almonds. Simmer covered for 15 minutes. Uncover and cook until juices are absorbed. Allow to cool.

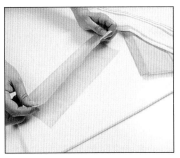

2 Position pastry with long side in front of you. Cut into 3 even 5-inch wide strips. Stack and cover with clean dishtowel. Take 2 strips at a time, spray each lightly with canola oil spray and fold in half, long side to long side. Spray surface with oil spray.

3 Place a teaspoon of filling on bottom end of each strip. Fold right-hand corner over to form a triangle then fold on the straight then on diagonal until end is reached. Repeat with remaining. Place on a baking sheet sprayed with oil. Spray tops of triangles with oil and bake in a preheated moderate oven for 20–25 minutes. Serve hot as finger food.

chicken and almond triangles

ingredients

1 tablespoon olive oil
60 g (2 oz) slivered almonds
1 medium onion, finely chopped
½ teaspoon salt
1 teaspoon ground cinnamon
1 teaspoon paprika
2 teaspoons ground cumin
500 g (1 lb) ground chicken
2 small tomatoes, chopped
45 g (1½ oz) raisins, chopped
2 tablespoons finely chopped
  flat-leaf parsley
4 tablespoons dry white wine
14 sheets filo pastry
canola oil spray
makes 42

1 Heat a heavy skillet. Add a teaspoon of the oil and sauté the almonds until pale gold in color. Quickly remove with a slotted spoon. Add remaining oil and the onion and fry until soft. Stir in salt, cinnamon, paprika and cumin and cook until aromatic. Add ground chicken and stir-fry until almost cooked. Add tomatoes, raisins, parsley, wine

i

preparation time
30 minutes

cooking time
48 minutes

**nutritional value
per serve**
fat: 8.6 g
carbohydrate: 12.2 g
protein: 10.6 g

curried chicken rolls

ingredients

2 teaspoons canola oil
1 medium onion, finely chopped
1 small clove garlic, minced
2 teaspoons mild curry paste
1 1/2 tablespoons lemon juice
500 g (1 lb) ground chicken
3 tablespoons dried breadcrumbs
1/2 teaspoon salt
1/2 teaspoon pepper
2 tablespoons chopped cilantro
2 sheets frozen puff pastry, thawed
1 tablespoon milk for glazing
1 tablespoon sesame seeds
serves 16–20

1 Heat oil in a small pan, add onion and garlic and fry until onion is soft. Stir in curry paste and cook a little. Add lemon juice and stir to mix. In a bowl, combine the chicken, breadcrumbs, salt, pepper and cilantro. Add the onion and curry mixture and combine well.

2 Preheat the oven to 190°C (370°F, gas mark 5). Cut each sheet of puff pastry in half across the center. Pile a 1/4 of the mixture in a thick half-inch wide strip along the center of each pastry strip. Brush the exposed pastry at the back with water.

3 Lift the front strip of pastry over the filling and roll to rest onto the back strip. Press lightly to seal.

4 Cut the roll into 4 or 5 equal portions. Repeat the process with the remaining chicken and pastry.

5 Glaze with milk and sprinkle with sesame seeds. Place onto a baking sheet. Cook in the preheated oven for 10 minutes, reduce heat to 180°C (350°F, gas mark 4) and continue cooking for 15 minutes until golden brown. Serve hot as finger food.

preparation time
20 minutes

cooking time
28 minutes

nutritional value per serve
fat: 13.1 g
carbohydrate: 14.1 g
protein: 11.9 g

chicken focaccia with marinated vegetables

ingredients

500 g (1 lb) chicken breast fillets
1 clove garlic, minced
salt and pepper to taste
1 tablespoon lemon juice
2 teaspoons olive oil
6 portions of focaccia bread either
    individual or slab
1 tablespoon olive oil
6 slices marinated roasted eggplant
    (aubergine)
100 g (3½ oz) marinated mushrooms
6 slices marinated roasted red
    bell pepper
makes 6

i

preparation time
8 minutes, plus
30 minutes
marinating

cooking time
7–8 minutes

**nutritional value
per serve**
fat: 4.6 g
carbohydrate: 19.3 g
protein: 10.1 g

1 In a non-metallic dish, place chicken breast fillets and add garlic, salt, pepper, lemon juice and oil. Cover and marinate for 30 minutes in the refrigerator. Heat a non-stick pan or greased broiler plate and sear the fillets for 1 minute on each side. Cook a further 2 minutes on each side. When cooked cut into diagonal slices. Keep hot.

2 Cut the focaccia slab into serving portions and split through the center. Brush cut surface with olive oil. Place a slice of eggplant on each base, arrange chicken slices on top and cover with mushrooms and bell peppers. Replace top slice. Place in a moderate oven at 160°C (325°F, gas mark 3) to heat for 10 minutes. Serve hot.

party
satay
wings

ingredients

1 kg (2 lb) chicken wings
satay sauce
185 g (6 oz) peanut butter
$^3/_4$ cup (185 ml, 6 fl oz) water
2 tablespoons brown sugar
$^1/_8$ teaspoon chilli powder
1 tablespoon soy sauce
1 tablespoon onion, grated
makes 32

1 In a saucepan, combine the peanut butter, water, sugar, chilli powder, soy sauce and onion. Heat and simmer for 5 minutes. Allow to cool.

2 Preheat oven to 180°C (350°F, gas mark 4). Rinse the wings and pat dry with paper towel. Cut off the wing tip and discard. Cut through next joint to make two pieces. Place all the wings in a bowl and stir through $^1/_2$ cup (125 ml, 4 fl oz) satay sauce. Cover and marinate, in the refrigerator, for 2 hours or overnight.

3 Arrange wing pieces underside upward on a rack over a shallow dish lined with foil. Bake in preheated oven for 15 minutes. Turn the wings and brush with the marinade sauce. Cook 20 minutes more. Brush again with marinade sauce, increase heat to 200°C (400°F, gas mark 6) and cook approximately 5 minutes more to crisp.

4 Remove from oven. Brush with 1 tablespoon fresh satay sauce (do not use the remaining marinade sauce) to intensify the flavor.

5 Arrange on platter and serve hot as finger food with fresh satay sauce to dip.

preparation time
10 minutes, plus 2 hours or overnight marinating

cooking time
45 minutes

nutritional value per serve
fat: 11.6 g
carbohydrate: 3.3 g
protein: 21.2 g

vindaloo chicken nuggets

ingredients

1 kg (2 lb) chicken thigh fillets
salt and pepper
1 tablespoon lemon juice
2 tablespoons vindaloo curry paste
125 g (4 oz) flour
2 eggs, lightly beaten
185 g (6½ oz) dried breadcrumbs
canola oil spray

yogurt and cucumber dipping sauce

1 lebanese cucumber, grated
1 cup (250 g, 8 oz) plain yogurt
1 clove garlic, minced
1 tablespoon lemon juice
salt and pepper to taste

makes 32

i

preparation time
20 minutes,
plus 2 hours
marinating.

cooking time
15-18 minutes

**nutritional value
per serve**
fat: 5.7 g
carbohydrate: 12.4 g
protein: 15.0 g

1 Cut each thigh fillet into 4 pieces. In a bowl, place fillets and sprinkle lightly with salt and pepper. Pour over 1 tablespoon lemon juice. Toss to mix through. Rub the vindaloo curry paste well into each piece with your fingers. Cover and refrigerate 2 hours or more.

2 Preheat oven to 200°C (400°F, gas mark 6). Into shallow dishes or trays, place the flour, egg and breadcrumbs. Coat the chicken nuggets in flour, dip into the egg and press into the breadcrumbs to coat all sides. Lightly spray a large baking sheet with canola oil spray. Place nuggets on the sheet and spray the tops. Cook in a preheated oven for 15–18 minutes.

3 Into a strainer, place the cucumber and press to drain off excess liquid. Mix into the yogurt. Add garlic, lemon juice, salt and pepper and place in a serving bowl. Serve with the hot nuggets.

lavish rolls

ingredients

1 kg (2 lb) chicken tenderloins
1 packet of 8 lavash flat breads
340 g (11$^{1}/_{2}$ oz) jar mayonnaise
1 small lettuce, shredded
$^{1}/_{2}$ bunch green onions,
  chopped
4 tomatoes, sliced
other vegetables of choice, eg,
  avocado, carrot (optional)
250 g (8 oz) tub of hummus
2 tablespoons lemon juice

serves 8

1 Spray a heated non-stick pan or broiler plate with oil spray and cook tenderloins for 2 minutes on each side.

2 Place in turn each lavash sheet on work surface. Spread lightly with mayonnaise. Sprinkle with shredded lettuce leaving the bottom 1.5 inches uncovered. Sprinkle green onions over the lettuce and place on tomato slices and other vegetables. Place 3–4 tenderloins down the center and drizzle with a little hummus diluted with lemon juice.

3 Turn up bottom edge to hold in the filling and roll from the side into a tight roll. Wrap bottom half in wax paper or foil and serve.

preparation time
20 minutes

cooking time
4 minutes

**nutritional value
per serve**
fat: 7.5 g
carbohydrate: 11.7 g
protein: 8.8 g

chicken party sticks

ingredients

500 g (2 lb) chicken tenderloins
salt and pepper to taste
2 packets frozen puff pastry sheets
1 cup (250 ml, 8 fl oz) of bottled satay
  or sweet chilli sauce
2 tablespoons milk
1 tablespoon poppy or sesame seeds
makes 32

1 Preheat oven to 180°C (350°F, gas mark 4). Sprinkle salt and pepper over the chicken. Cut sheet of thawed pastry into 4 squares. Place a chicken tenderloin on each square and add a dash of your chosen sauce. Roll up on the diagonal, leaving ends open. Place seam-side down on a baking sheet and glaze with milk. Sprinkle with poppy or sesame seeds.

2 Bake in preheated oven for 25–30 minutes. Serve hot as finger food with same sauce used as a dipping sauce.

i

preparation time
15 minutes

cooking time
25-30 minutes

**nutritional value
per serve**
fat: 18.3 g
carbohydrate: 25.2 g
protein: 9.2 g

spicy chicken burritos

ingredients

500 g (1 lb) chicken stir-fry
1 tablespoon olive oil
1 large onion, finely chopped
1 clove garlic, minced
180 g (6 oz) tomato and
  garlic pasta sauce
$\frac{1}{2}$ teaspoon chilli powder
1 packet of 12 mexican tortillas

topping

1 tub guacamole
2 large onions, thinly sliced
1 carton sour cream
350 g (11$\frac{1}{2}$ oz) cheddar cheese, grated
420 g (14 oz) can refried beans, heated
  (optional)

makes 32

preparation time
10 minutes

cooking time
18 minutes

**nutritional value
per serve**
fat: 11.4 g
carbohydrate: 7.6 g
protein: 9.5 g

1 Chop the stir-fry into smaller pieces. Heat the oil in a large skillet. Add onions and garlic and fry until soft. Add the chicken and stir to brown on all sides. Stir in tomato pasta sauce and chilli powder. Simmer for 15 minutes or until chicken is cooked and sauce thickens.

2 Prepare the toppings and place in suitable serving dishes. Heat a large skillet, place in a tortilla and heat for 40 seconds on each side. Remove and place on a clean towel and cover. Heat remainder and stack in towel.

3 On each tortilla spread a portion of chicken mixture and top with toppings of choice. Roll up and serve immediately.

broiled
chicken

chicken and mushroom patties

ingredients

500 g (1 lb) ground chicken
60 g (2 oz) dried breadcrumbs
1 medium onion, finely chopped
1/2 teaspoon salt
1/2 teaspoon pepper
2 tablespoons lemon juice
2 tablespoons chopped parsley
45 g (1 1/2 oz) finely chopped mushrooms
vegetable oil

serves 4-6

i

preparation time
10 minutes

cooking time
16 minutes

nutritional value
per serve
fat: 7.0 g
carbohydrate: 6.2 g
protein: 14.2 g

1 In a large bowl, place ground chicken, breadcrumbs, onion, salt, pepper, lemon juice, parsley and mushrooms. Mix well to combine ingredients. Knead a little with one hand to make the chicken fine in texture. With wet hands, shape into 4–5 flat patties.

2 Heat barbecue or broiler to medium-high. Oil the broiler bars or rack with a little vegetable oil and place on patties. Cook for 8 minutes on each side or until cooked through. Serve hot with vegetable accompaniments. May be served with barbecue sauce.

char-grilled chicken with mango salsa

ingredients

4 chicken breast fillets
2 tablespoons thai fish sauce
juice of ½ lime
salt and black pepper
1 tablespoon olive oil
fresh mint to garnish
lime wedges to serve

salsa
½ red bell pepper,
   seeded and quartered
1 mango, chopped
1 small red chilli pepper, seeded and
   finely chopped
1 tablespoon olive oil
juice of ½ lime
1 tablespoon chopped cilantro
1 tablespoon chopped fresh mint
salt and pepper

serves 4

1 Place the chicken breasts between cling film and pound with a rolling pin to flatten them slightly. Unwrap and place in a non-metallic dish. In a small bowl, combine the fish sauce, lime juice, salt and pepper and pour over the chicken. Cover and leave to marinate in the refrigerator for 1 hour.

2 Preheat the broiler to high. Broil the bell pepper skin side up until it blisters. Peel off the skin and dice. In a bowl, combine the mango, bell pepper, chilli pepper, oil, lime juice, cilantro, mint, salt and pepper. Cover and refrigerate.

3 Heat the tablespoon of oil in a large heavy skillet. Add the chicken and fry for 3–4 minutes on each side. Pour over any remaining marinade and cook until chicken is cooked through. Remove to a serving plate. Serve with mango salsa and garnish with mint and lime.

preparation time
20 minutes,
plus 1 hour
marinating

cooking time
20 minutes

**nutritional value
per serve**
fat: 6.3 g
carbohydrate: 1.8 g
protein: 16.9 g

southern barbecued chicken

This recipe needs to be cooked on a barbecue with a lid or hood for best results.

ingredients

2 kg (4 lb) fresh chicken cut into pieces
jacket potatoes
southern barbecue sauce
350 ml (11 1/2 fl oz) can tomato purée
1 cup (250 ml, 8 fl oz) cider vinegar
1/2 cup (125 ml, 4 fl oz) canola oil
1/3 cup (80 ml, 2 1/2 fl oz) worcestershire sauce
75 g (2 1/2 oz) brown sugar
4 tablespoons molasses
2 tablespoons french-style mustard
2-3 cloves garlic, minced
4 tablespoons lemon juice
serves 6-8

1 Into a saucepan, place tomato purée, cider vinegar, canola oil, worcestershire sauce, brown sugar, mustard, garlic and lemon juice. Stir to combine. Bring to a simmer and continue to simmer over low heat for 15–20 minutes, stirring regularly. Stand for 1 hour to cool and to allow flavors to blend.

2 Cut chicken into 6–8 serving pieces. Heat barbecue to moderate and oil the bars. Lightly sear chicken pieces on

all sides over direct heat about 2 minutes each side, remove to a plate.

3 Place half the sauce into a small pan and place by the barbecue. Place a sheet of silicon baking paper over the bars and prick at intervals between the runs to allow ventilation. Place the chicken onto the baking paper and brush all over with the sauce.

4 Cover barbecue with the lid and cook for 5 minutes, lift the lid, brush chicken with sauce, turn and brush with sauce, close lid and cook 5 minutes. Repeat this process every 5 minutes for 40–45 minutes until chicken is rich brown in color and cooked through. If chicken is cooking too quickly, reduce heat by turning down gas or rake the coals to the sides. Heat remaining sauce in a small saucepan on the barbecue.

5 Serve chicken with hot sauce and jacket potatoes cooked on the barbecue. Accompany with a salad.

i

preparation time
10 minutes

cooking time
40 minutes, plus
1 hour standing

nutritional value per serve
fat: 5.8 g
carbohydrate: 10.3 g
protein: 7.6 g

broiled sesame chicken with ginger rice

ingredients

500 (1 lb) chicken tenderloin
soy and honey marinade
1 tablespoon sesame seeds, toasted
1 tablespoon rice wine (mirin) or sherry
2 teaspoons honey or plum sauce
2 teaspoons soy sauce
2 teaspoons oyster sauce
1 teaspoon sesame oil
ginger rice
1 tablespoon finely chopped fresh ginger
1 teaspoon sesame oil
1 cup (220 g, 7½ oz) short-grain rice,
   rinsed and drained
330 ml (11 fl oz) ginger beer
1 tablespoon pickled or preserved ginger
1 green onion, finely chopped
serves 4

1 In a non-metallic bowl, place sesame seeds, wine, honey, soy and oyster sauces and sesame oil. Mix to combine. Add chicken and toss to coat. Cover and marinate in the refrigerator for at least 1 hour.

2 Place fresh ginger and sesame oil in a large saucepan over a low heat. Cook, stirring occasionally, for 5 minutes. Add rice. Cook, stirring, for 2 minutes. Stir in ginger beer and pickled ginger. Bring to the boil. Reduce heat and cover. Simmer for 10–15 minutes or until liquid is absorbed and rice is cooked. Stir in green onion.

3 Preheat broiler or barbecue to a medium heat. Lightly oil the bars and place on the tenderloins. Cook for 3–4 minutes on each side, brushing regularly with marinade. Serve chicken with ginger rice.

preparation time
5 minutes
cooking time
25 minutes
nutritional value per serve
fat: 2.6 g
carbohydrate: 30 g
protein: 3 g

broiled chicken tenderloins with spiced pumpkin

ingredients

500 g (1 lb) chicken tenderloins
2 tablespoons lemon juice
1 clove garlic, minced
2 teaspoons olive oil
salt and pepper
250 g (8 oz) potatoes, peeled, cut
   and rinsed
500 g (1 lb) pumpkin, cut and peeled
2 tablespoons milk
1 teaspoon nutmeg
1 tablespoon chopped cilantro
   or parsley
canola oil spray
1 medium onion, thinly sliced
2 medium tomatoes, sliced

serves 4

i

preparation time
10 minutes,
plus 40 minutes
marinating

cooking time
20 minutes

nutritional value
fat: 2.9 g
carbohydrate: 4.5 g
protein: 7.3 g

1 In a non-metallic dish, place tenderloins. Add lemon juice, garlic and oil. Cover and marinate 40 minutes in the refrigerator. In a saucepan, boil the potato and pumpkin until tender, drain and mash. Add the milk, nutmeg and cilantro or parsley. Set aside and keep hot.

2 Heat preferred broiler to high and spray lightly with canola oil spray. On the broiler, put the tenderloins, onion and tomatoes. Cook tenderloins for 2 minutes each, turn the tomatoes and onions and cook till soft.

3 Pile the spiced pumpkin onto 4 heated plates. Arrange the tenderloins over the pumpkin and top with broiled tomato and onion.

chicken kebabs with couscous

ingredients

4 chicken breast fillets
1 red bell pepper, seeded and
    cut into 8 pieces
1 yellow bell pepper, seeded and cut
    into 8 pieces
juice of 1 lemon
2 garlic cloves, minced
2 tablespoons extra virgin olive oil
1 tablespoon chopped fresh cilantro
2 tablespoons butter
4 green onions, finely
    chopped
250 g (8 oz) instant couscous
3 tablespoons chopped cilantro
salt and pepper
1 cup (250 ml, 8 fl oz) boiling water
sauce
150 g (5 oz) natural yogurt
1 tablespoon lemon juice
1 teaspoon grated lemon rind
salt to taste
freshly ground black pepper
serves 4

i

preparation time
30 minutes, plus
1 hour marinating

cooking time
15 minutes

**nutritional value
per serve**
fat: 6.9 g
carbohydrate: 9.7 g
protein: 15.4 g

1 Cut each fillet into 4–6 pieces depending on size. Place in a non-metallic bowl. Add the bell peppers, lemon juice, garlic, olive oil and cilantro and toss to coat. Cover and leave to marinate for at least 1 hour. Soak four large wooden skewers in water for about 10 minutes.

2 Melt the butter in a small saucepan and fry the green onions for about 2 minutes. Add the couscous, cilantro, salt, pepper and boiling water, and stir to combine. Cover and set aside. In a bowl, combine sauce ingredients and chill until needed.

3 Preheat the broiler to high. Thread the chicken and bell peppers onto the skewers and broil for 10–12 minutes, turning occasionally, until the chicken is lightly browned and cooked through.

4 Fluff up the couscous with a fork. Pile onto 4 plates and place kebabs on top. Drizzle over the yogurt sauce.

citrus and spice broiled chicken

ingredients

1 kg (2 lb) fresh chicken
zest of 1 orange (optional)

marinade

½ cup (125 ml, 4 fl oz) cider vinegar
½ cup (125 ml, 4 fl oz) orange juice
½ cup (125 ml, 4 fl oz) grapefruit juice
1 teaspoon cinnamon
½ teaspoon ground nutmeg
1 teaspoon sugar
½ teaspoon salt (optional)

serves 2-4

1 With a cleaver or large sharp knife, cut chicken through the breastbone and open out. Cut on each side of the backbone discarding it, forming 2 halves.

i

preparation time
10 minutes, plus 12 hours or overnight marinating

cooking time
32 minutes

nutritional value per serve
fat: 4.4 g
carbohydrate: 1.7 g
protein: 14.3 g

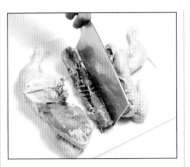

2 Mix marinade ingredients together. In a non-metallic flat dish, place chicken halves and pour over the marinade. Cover and refrigerate for 12 hours or overnight, turning occasionally.

3 Heat oven broiler element or gas broiler to medium. Place chicken halves in the pan under the broiler. Cook for 10 minutes on each side brushing frequently with marinade. Lift chicken onto rack so as to come closer to heat, cook 5 minutes on each side. Turn heat to high and cook about 2 minutes to brown and crisp. Remove chicken to a heated platter.

4 Skim the fat from the pan juices and pour juices over the chicken. Serve hot with vegetable accompaniments. Garnish with strips of orange rind (optional).

spicy satay skewers

1 Mix all satay sauce ingredients together in a saucepan, heat to simmer, then simmer for 5 minutes. Remove from heat and allow to cool.

2 Cut thigh fillets in half down the center. Cut the thinner side into 2 and the thicker side into 3 pieces. Place in a bowl and sprinkle with salt, pepper, lemon juice and garlic, stir to mix through. Pour marinade over chicken, cover and stand to marinate in the refrigerator for at least 1 hour or leave overnight in the refrigerator.

3 Soak bamboo skewers in water. Thread 4–5 pieces onto each skewer until just touching. If pushed too close together, the center will not cook sufficiently.

4 Broil or barbecue on moderately high heat for 10–12 minutes turning frequently and brushing with sauce. Remove to platter and sprinkle with toasted sesame seeds. Serve with remaining satay sauce.

ingredients
500 g (1 lb) thigh fillets
salt and pepper
1 tablespoon lemon juice
1 clove garlic, minced
satay sauce
180 g (6 fl oz) peanut butter
3/4 cup (180 ml, 6 fl oz) water
2 tablespoons brown sugar
1/8 teaspoon chilli powder, or to taste
1 tablespoon soy sauce
1 tablespoon grated onion
2 tablespoons toasted sesame seeds
bamboo skewers, soaked
serves 4-5

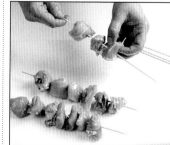

preparation time
8 minutes, plus
1 hour or
overnight
marinating

cooking time
15 minutes

**nutritional value
per serve**
fat: 17.8 g
carbohydrate: 5.5 g
protein: 18.8 g

chicken
salads

chicken waldorf

ingredients

400 g (13 oz) chicken breast fillets
1 onion, roughly chopped
1 carrot, roughly chopped
pinch of salt
2 red apples
1 tablespoon lemon juice
2 stalks celery, diced
60 g (2 oz) blonde walnuts, coarsely
  chopped
125 g (4 oz) mayonnaise
1 lettuce, separated into cups, washed
  and crisped

serves 6-8

1 To poach the chicken fillets: place fillets, onion, carrot and salt in a pan and add hot water just to cover. Bring to a simmer, reduce heat and simmer gently for 20 minutes. Turn off heat and cool in its juices. Strain, reserve stock for future use.

2 Cut chicken into half-inch cubes. Wash apples well, leave skin on and cut into half-inch cubes. Sprinkle with lemon juice.

3 In a bowl, toss chicken, apples, celery and walnuts together. Add mayonnaise and gently toss through. Spoon into the lettuce cups and serve as an appetizer or light lunch; or line a salad bowl with lettuce leaves and pile salad into the center and serve for a buffet.

i

preparation time
10 minutes

cooking time
20 minutes

**nutritional value
per serve**
fat: 6.3 g
carbohydrate: 4.5 g
protein: 6.2 g

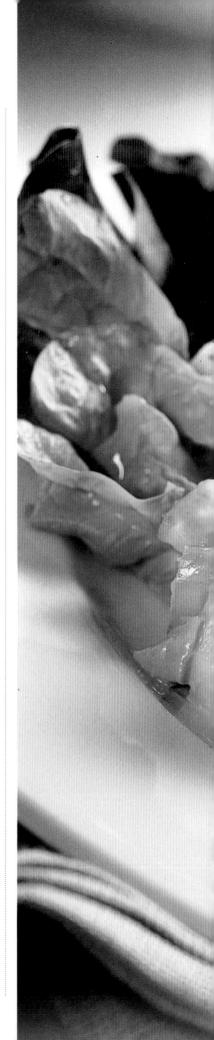

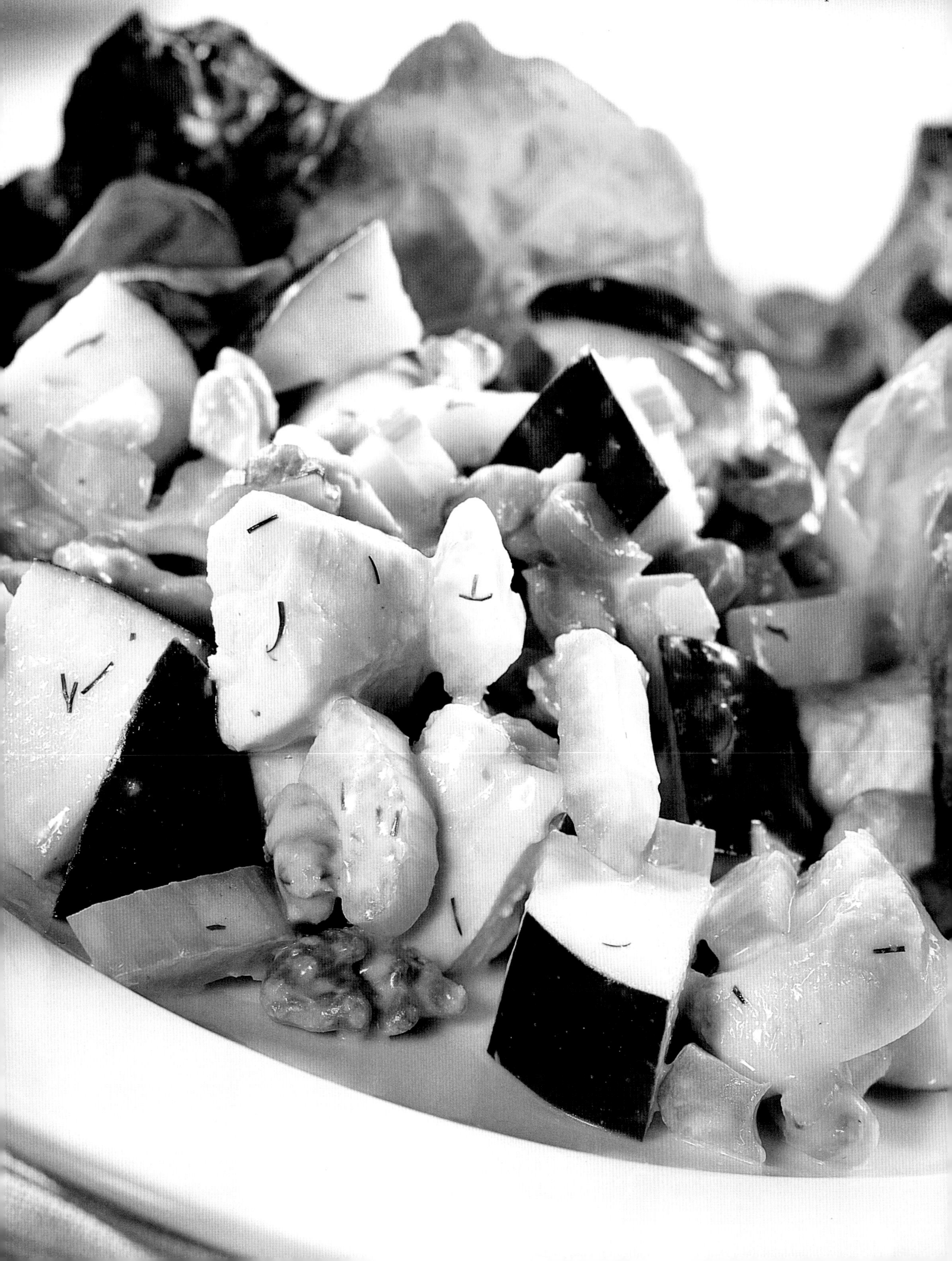

chicken and endive salad with creamy dressing

ingredients

1 slender french bread stick (baguette)
1 clove garlic, minced
2 tablespoons oil
1 bunch curly endive
4 green onions, sliced
250 g (8 oz) can mandarin orange segments, drained and juice reserved
250 g (8 oz) chicken tenderloins
dressing
250 ml (8 fl oz) coleslaw dressing
1 teaspoon dijon mustard
serves 4

1 Cut bread stick into quater-inch slices. Mix garlic and oil together and brush onto bread slices. Place on a tray in oven and cook at 180°C (350°F, gas mark 4) until crisp and golden. Break endive into 2-inch pieces. In a bowl, toss together endive, green onions and mandarin orange segments.

2 Cook tenderloins in a lightly greased non-stick pan for 2 minutes on each side. Mound the bread and endive salad onto individual serving plates and arrange chicken on top. Combine coleslaw dressing and mustard and drizzle over the salad. Serve as an appetizer.

preparation time
10 minutes

cooking time
10 minutes

nutritional value per serve
fat: 9.1 g
carbohydrate: 22.6 g
protein: 6.5 g

1 Wash greens, drain and dry. Tear leaves into pieces and place into a large bowl. Toss in apple slices and half of the walnuts.

tossed greens and chicken with blue cheese dressing

ingredients

1 bunch rocket leaves
1 coral lettuce
1 mignonette lettuce
1 red apple, cored, thinly sliced, splashed with lemon juice
60 g (2 oz) pale walnut pieces
2 poached chicken breasts
60 g (2 oz) extra blue-vein cheese for topping

dressing

4 tablespoons olive oil
2 tablespoons white-wine vinegar
1 tablespoon lemon juice
1/4 teaspoon sugar
1 tablespoon dijon mustard
30 g (1 oz) blue-vein cheese, crumbled
pinch cayenne

serves 4-6

i

preparation time
15 minutes

nutritional value
per serve
fat: 10.5 g
carbohydrate: 1.9 g
protein: 6.5 g

2 Cut the chicken into diagonal slices and add to salad greens. Beat the dressing ingredients together and pour over salad. Sprinkle top with remaining walnuts and extra crumbled blue-vein cheese. Serve as an appetizer or lunch dish.

hot chicken ball salad with fruity dressing

ingredients

500 g (1 lb) ground chicken
$^1/_2$ teaspoon salt
$^1/_2$ teaspoon pepper
2 tablespoons dried breadcrumbs
1 medium onion, very finely chopped
2 tablespoons finely chopped parsley
1 tablespoon lemon juice
1 egg
3 tablespoons flour for dusting
oil for frying
500 g (1 lb) mixed salad greens

fruity dressing

4 tablespoons cider vinegar
1 tablespoon mustard powder
1 tablespoon soy sauce
450 g (14 oz) can pineapple pieces
2 large bananas, sliced
2 tablespoons cornstarch, blended with
  2 tablespoons cold water

serves 6

1 In a bowl, combine the chicken with the salt, pepper, breadcrumbs, onion, parsley, lemon juice and egg. Knead for 2 minutes with a gloved hand to make a fine-grained mixture.

2 Take tablespoons of the mixture and roll into balls with wet hands.

3 Heat enough oil to be about quater of an inch deep in the skillet. Roll the chicken balls in flour, shake off excess. Add a third of the balls and fry, rolling them around to cook all sides. Remove and drain on paper towels. Cook remainder.

4 In a saucepan, place vinegar, mustard and soy sauce. Add the juice from the pineapple pieces and blend in the cornstarch. Stir over heat until the sauce thickens and boils. Add the pineapple pieces, bananas, chicken balls and heat through. Pile salad greens on individual plates or a platter and spoon on the chicken balls and sauce. Serve immediately.

preparation time
25 minutes

cooking time
8 minutes

**nutritional value
per serve**
fat: 12.1 g
carbohydrate: 6.9 g
protein: 5.4 g

party avocado and chicken salad

ingredients

1 kg (2 lb) chicken breast fillets, poached
3 avocados
1 tablespoon lemon juice
2 stalks celery, thinly sliced
60 g (2 oz) slivered almonds, toasted
1/2 green bell pepper cut into slices
420 g (14 oz) can mango slices, drained
1 cucumber, sliced
lettuce leaves for serving

dressing
1 cup (250 ml, 8 fl oz) heavy cream, whipped
125 g (4 oz) mayonnaise
1/2 nutmeg, grated
1 teaspoon paprika
salt and pepper

serves 10–20

preparation time
15 minutes

cooking time
15 minutes

nutritional value per serve
fat: 13.4 g
carbohydrate: 3.3 g
protein: 9.6 g

1 Poach the chicken, cool then cut into large cubes. Peel the avocados and cut two into large cubes and the third into slices for garnish. Sprinkle slices with lemon juice.

2 Combine the chicken, celery, almonds, bell pepper and avocado cubes. Reserve a few mango and cucumber slices for garnish and toss remainder into the salad.

3 In a bowl, combine dressing ingredients. Pour over the salad and toss gently. Arrange lettuce leaves on a shallow platter. Pile on the chicken mixture. Garnish with reserved avocado, mango and cucumber.

curried chicken salad

ingredients

1 large cooked barbecued chicken
2 stalks celery, finely chopped
6 green onions, sliced
60 g (2 oz) raisins, soaked
60 g (2 oz) slivered almonds, toasted
200 g (7 oz) mixed salad greens,
   washed and crisped
1 mango, sliced to garnish
2 tablespoons shredded coconut,
   toasted to garnish

dressing

150 g (5 oz) mayonnaise
150 g (5 oz) low-fat yogurt
3 tablespoons sweet mango chutney
1 tablespoon mild curry paste
2 tablespoons lemon juice
2 teaspoons freshly grated
   lemon zest

serves 8

1 Remove the chicken meat from the bones and cut into bite-size pieces. Toss with the celery, green onions, raisins and almonds.

2 In a bowl, place all dressing ingredients and beat until smooth. Pour over chicken, toss to mix through. Cover and chill 2 hours or more.

3 Line platter or individual plates with salad greens and pile on the chicken mixture. Garnish with mango slices and sprinkle with toasted, shredded coconut.

i

preparation time
10 minutes,
plus 2 hours
refrigeration

**nutritional value
per serve**
fat: 9.1 g
carbohydrate: 7.2 g
protein: 10.3 g

marinated chicken salad

ingredients

2 cups (500 ml, 16 fl oz) oil
500 g (1 lb) chicken stir-fry
60 g (2 oz) flour seasoned with salt and pepper
4 tablespoons orange juice
4 tablespoons olive oil
1 tablespoon chopped mint
$^1/_2$ teaspoon salt
freshly ground black pepper
1 avocado, sliced
425 g (14 oz) can apricots
1 container snow pea sprouts

serves 6–8

i

preparation time
10 minutes,
plus 30 minutes
marinating

cooking time
5 minutes

nutritional value per serve
fat: 15 g
carbohydrate: 6.4 g
protein: 7.3 g

1 Heat oil in a deep skillet. Dip the stir-fry strips in the flour a few at a time and deep-fry in the hot oil until cooked and golden in color. Drain on paper towels and place in a glass bowl.

2 Combine orange juice, oil, mint, salt and pepper in a screw-top jar and shake well. Pour over chicken strips and refrigerate for a minimum of 30 minutes.

3 Slice avocado and drain apricot halves, reserving 2 tablespoons of juice from the can. Arrange snow pea sprouts on individual plates. Top with chicken strips, avocado pieces and apricot halves. Add about 1–2 teaspoons juice to remaining marinade and drizzle over salad. Serve as an appetizer or as a lunch dish with crusty bread.

pan-fried chicken

chicken breasts with shiitake mushrooms

ingredients

6 chicken breast fillets
2 tablespoons peanut oil
1 onion, chopped
2-inch piece fresh root ginger, finely chopped
200 g (7 oz) shiitake mushrooms, stems removed and caps sliced
150 g (5 oz) baby button mushrooms
2 tablespoons dark soy sauce
300 ml (10 fl oz) chicken stock
200 ml (7 fl oz) dry white wine
350 g (11½ oz) small zucchini, trimmed and sliced
cilantro, chopped to garnish

serves 4

i

preparation time
15 minutes

cooking time
50 minutes

nutritional value per serve
fat: 4.5 g
carbohydrate: 0.6 g
protein: 13.5 g

1 Make 3 slashes in each chicken breast, using a sharp knife. Heat the oil in a large, heavy-based saucepan or skillet with lid. Add the chicken and fry for 2–3 minutes on each side to brown. Remove to a plate.

2 Add the onion and ginger to the pan, fry until the onion has softened. Add both the mushrooms and the soy sauce and cook for a further 4–5 minutes.

3 Stir in the stock and wine and the zucchini slices. Bring to the boil then quickly turn down to a simmer. Return the chicken to the pan, cover and simmer for 15–20 minutes until chicken is cooked through. Sprinkle with cilantro and serve with rice or asian noodles.

italian chicken in a pan

1 Place chicken between sheets of wax paper and pound lightly to flatten. Dust with flour, then dip in egg and finally coat with breadcrumbs. Place on a plate lined with plastic food wrap, cover and refrigerate for 15 minutes.

2 Heat oil in a large skillet pan over a medium heat. Add chicken and cook for 2–3 minutes each side or until golden. Remove from pan and set aside. Pour off the oil and wipe the pan with paper towels. Add pasta sauce to pan stirring over a medium heat until hot.

3 Place chicken in a single layer on top of sauce, then top each fillet with a slice of prosciutto or ham, a slice of cheese and a sprig of sage. Cover and simmer for 5 minutes or until chicken is cooked through and cheese melts. Serve immediately.

ingredients

6 chicken breast fillets
flour seasoned with salt and pepper
1 egg, beaten
dried breadcrumbs
4 tablespoons vegetable oil
500 g (1 lb) jar tomato pasta sauce
6 slices prosciutto or ham
6 slices mozzarella cheese
6 sprigs fresh sage
serves 6

i

preparation time
15 minutes,
plus 15 minutes
refrigeration

cooking time
15 minutes

**nutritional value
per serve**
fat: 7.2 g
carbohydrate: 5.4 g
protein: 16.9 g

tangy tenderloins

ingredients

500 g (1 lb) chicken tenderloins
salt and pepper
olive oil spray
200 g (7 oz) sugar snap peas
425 g (14 oz) can baby corn, drained
½ cup (125 ml, 4 fl oz) apricot nectar
2 tablespoons sweet chilli sauce
2 tablespoons cider vinegar
serves 5

1 Flatten the tenderloins slightly and sprinkle with salt and pepper. Heat a heavy skillet and spray lightly with oil spray. Add tenderloins and cook 2 minutes on each side. Remove from pan.

2 Add the sugar snap peas and stir until they brighten in color. Add the corn. Return the chicken to the pan and toss with the vegetables. In a bowl, combine the apricot nectar, sweet chilli sauce and vinegar. Pour over chicken and vegetables and heat through. Pile onto serving plates. Serve immediately.

i

preparation time
10 minutes

cooking time
10 minutes

nutritional value per serve
fat: 3.2 g
carbohydrate: 8.4 g
protein: 9.4 g

poached chicken with tomato and mushroom sauce

ingredients

1 medium-sized onion, finely chopped
1 clove garlic, finely chopped
3 large ripe tomatoes, blanched, peeled and chopped
100 g (3½ oz) mushrooms, sliced
1 tablespoon chopped fresh basil
¾ cup (185 ml, 6 fl oz) water
1 teaspoon dried oregano
freshly ground black pepper
2 chicken breast fillets
60 g (2 oz) pasta twists
1.5 litres (2½ pints) boiling water
½ teaspoon olive oil
parmesan cheese, grated to serve

serves 2–3

ℹ

preparation time
10 minutes

cooking time
20 minutes

nutritional value per serve
fat: 3.6 g
carbohydrate: 3.9 g
protein: 11.8 g

1 Place onion, garlic, tomatoes and mushrooms in a heavy saucepan over moderate heat. Stir until they begin to soften. Add basil, water, oregano and pepper. Heat a little and add the chicken. Cover and simmer slowly for 20 minutes until chicken is tender. Do not allow to boil.

2 In another saucepan cook pasta twists in boiling water for 16–18 minutes. Drain and stir the olive oil through.

3 When chicken is cooked remove to a plate. If sauce is too thin, turn up heat and boil until it reduces and thickens. Pour over chicken and serve with pasta twists. Sprinkle with parmesan cheese.

chicken rogan josh

ingredients

1 tablespoon vegetable oil
1 small green bell pepper,
    thinly sliced
1 small red bell pepper, thinly sliced
1 onion, thinly sliced
2-inch piece of fresh root ginger,
    finely chopped
2 cloves garlic, minced
2 tablespoons garam masala
1 teaspoon paprika
1 teaspoon turmeric
1 teaspoon chilli powder
4 cardamom pods, crushed
salt to taste
8 chicken thigh fillets, each cut into
    4 pieces
200 g (7 oz) natural yogurt
400 g (13 oz) can chopped tomatoes
200 ml (7 fl oz) water
cilantro to garnish
mango chutney to serve
steamed rice to serve
serves 4

1 Heat the oil in a heavy skillet. Add the bell peppers, onion, ginger, garlic, spices and salt. Cover and fry over a low heat for 5 minutes or until the peppers and onion have softened.

2 Add the chicken and stir until it changes color. Stir in the yogurt and cook gently for 5 minutes.

3 Stir in the tomatoes and water and bring to the boil. Reduce the heat, cover, and simmer for 30 minutes or until the chicken is tender, stirring occasionally and adding more water if the sauce becomes too dry. Sprinkle with cilantro. Serve with steamed rice and mango chutney.

i

preparation time
15 minutes

cooking time
1 hour

**nutritional value
per serve**
fat: 4.9 g
carbohydrate: 1 g
protein: 16.6 g

chicken rolls with an indonesian flavor

1 Flatten the thigh fillets with a meat mallet to an even thinness. Spread each with a teaspoon of rendang curry sauce. Peel bananas and slit in half lengthwise then cut in half to make 4 pieces. Place a piece of banana in center of each fillet and form into a roll. Fasten with a toothpick.

4 Remove rolls to a heated platter and keep hot. If sauce is thin, increase heat and reduce sauce to a thicker consistency. Reduce heat and stir in the coconut milk, simmer 2 minutes. Return rolls to the saucepan to reheat.

2 Heat oil in a saucepan and brown the rolls on all sides, a few at a time, removing rolls to a plate as they brown.

5 Saute the pineapple rings in a little butter until lightly colored and grind over some black pepper. Arrange a slice of pineapple and a chicken roll on each plate, spoon sauce over the roll and sprinkle with a little toasted coconut. Accompany with steamed rice.

ingredients

1 kg (2 lb) chicken thigh fillets
290 g (10 oz) can redang curry sauce
2 bananas
toothpicks
2 tablespoons vegetable oil
1/2 cup (125 ml, 4 fl oz) water
150 ml (5 fl oz) coconut milk
1 small pineapple, peeled and thinly sliced
freshly ground black pepper
2 tablespoons shredded coconut, toasted
steamed rice to serve
serves 4

preparation time
15 minutes

cooking time
45 minutes

nutritional value per serve
fat: 7.6 g
carbohydrate: 4.8 g
protein: 10.6 g

3 Drain all the oil from the saucepan and add rendang curry sauce and the water. Bring to the boil, turn down heat to a simmer and place in the chicken rolls. Cover and simmer 35 minutes, turning rolls once during cooking.

hawaiian poached chicken

ingredients

1.5 kg (3 lb) chicken casserole pieces
1/2 teaspoon salt
1/2 teaspoon pepper
1 teaspoon paprika
2 tablespoons oil
1 large onion, chopped
1 clove garlic, minced
4 tablespoons water
1 tablespoon worcestershire sauce
2 teaspoons sweet chilli sauce
4 tablespoons apple cider vinegar
1 1/2 tablespoons brown sugar
1/2 medium fresh pineapple, peeled
   and diced
1 green bell pepper, seeded and
   cut into thin strips
1 red bell pepper, seeded and cut into
   thin strips
1 tablespoon rum (optional)
1 1/2 tablespoons cornstarch
boiled rice to serve

serves 6

i

preparation time
15 minutes,

cooking time
40 minutes

**nutritional value
per serve**
fat: 5.5 g
carbohydrate: 3.2 g
protein: 13.4 g

1 Season the chicken pieces with salt, pepper and paprika. Heat the oil in a large saucepan. Add chicken pieces a few at a time and brown on all sides. Remove to a plate lined with paper towels as they brown. Drain the oil from the saucepan.

2 Add the onion and garlic to the saucepan and cook, stirring for 2 minutes. Return chicken to the saucepan. In a bowl, combine the water, worcestershire sauce, sweet chilli sauce, vinegar and brown sugar and pour over the chicken. Add the pineapple pieces and bell peppers. Simmer for 30–35 minutes until chicken is tender.

3 Add the rum to the chicken. Blend the cornstarch and water together. Add the cornstarch to the chicken and stir through. Allow to simmer until it thickens. Increase the heat until it boils then turn off immediately. Serve with boiled rice.

spanish chicken with chorizo

ingredients

8 chicken pieces, thighs and drumsticks
2 tablespoons olive oil
1 onion, sliced
2 cloves garlic, minced
1 red bell pepper, seeded
    and sliced
1 yellow capsicum, seeded and sliced
2 teaspoons paprika
60 ml (2 fl oz) dry sherry or dry vermouth
400 g (13 oz) can chopped tomatoes
1 bay leaf
1 strip orange zest, pared with a
    vegetable peeler
75 g (2¹/₂ oz) chorizo sausage, sliced
60 g (2 oz) pitted black olives
salt and black pepper
serves 4

preparation time
15 minutes

cooking time
1 hour

**nutritional value
per serve**
fat: 5.3 g
carbohydrate: 1.7 g
protein: 12.5 g

1 Place the chicken joints in a large non-stick skillet and fry without oil for 5–8 minutes, turning occasionally, until golden. Remove the chicken and set aside, then wipe the pan clean with paper towels.

2 Add the oil to the pan and fry the onion, garlic and bell peppers for 3–4 minutes, until softened. Return the chicken to the pan with the paprika, sherry or vermouth, tomatoes, bay leaf and orange zest. Bring to the boil. Simmer, covered, over a low heat for 35–40 minutes stirring occasionally, until the chicken is cooked through.

3 Add the chorizo and olives and simmer for a further 5 minutes to heat through, then season. Serve with crusty bread and a side salad.

thai-spiced chicken with zucchini

ingredients

350 g (11½ oz) chicken breast fillets
1 tablespoon olive oil
1 clove garlic, finely chopped
2.5 cm fresh root ginger, finely chopped
1 small fresh red chilli pepper, seeded and finely chopped
1 tablespoon thai seven-spice seasoning
1 red bell pepper, seeded and sliced
1 yellow bell pepper, seeded and sliced
2 small zucchini, thinly sliced
250 g (8 oz) can bamboo shoots, drained
2 tablespoons dry sherry or apple juice
1 tablespoon light soy sauce
black pepper
2 tablespoons chopped cilantro
extra cilantro to garnish
hot noodles to serve
serves 4

preparation time
15 minutes

cooking tme
10 minutes

nutritional value per serve
fat: 4.5 g
carbohydrate: 1.8 g
protein: 7.9 g

1 With a sharp knife cut the chicken breasts into thin stir-fry strips.

2 Heat the oil in a non-stick wok or large skillet. Add the garlic, ginger and chilli pepper and stir-fry for 30 seconds to release the flavors. Add the chicken and thai seasoning and stir-fry for 4 minutes or until the chicken has colored. Add the bell peppers and zucchini and stir-fry for 1–2 minutes, until slightly softened.

3 Stir in the bamboo shoots and stir-fry for another 2–3 minutes, until the chicken is cooked through and tender. Add the sherry or apple juice, soy sauce and black pepper and sizzle for 1–2 minutes. Remove from the heat and stir in the chopped cilantro. Garnish with more cilantro and serve with hot noodles.

chicken with tomato vinaigrette

ingredients

4 chicken breast fillets
salt and black pepper
2 tablespoons balsamic vinegar
1 tablespoon tomato paste
175 ml (6 fl oz) dry white wine or
    chicken stock
1 tablespoon olive oil
½ teaspoon sugar
serves 4

1 Flatten the chicken breasts slightly with the side of a meat mallet and season with salt and pepper. In a jug, mix together the vinegar and tomato paste. Add the wine or stock, stirring to mix thoroughly. Set aside.

2 Heat the oil in a large heavy skillet. Add the chicken and cook for 2 minutes on each side. Add the vinaigrette, cook for 4–5 minutes, basting frequently and turning once, until the chicken is cooked through.

3 Transfer the chicken to a board and slice diagonally. Cover and keep warm. Add the sugar to the pan juices and boil until reduced by half. Plate the chicken and spoon over the vinaigrette. Serve with polenta and a leafy green salad.

i

preparation time
10 minutes

cooking time
15 minutes

nutritional value
per serve
fat: 5.7 g
carbohydrate: 0.4 g
protein: 18 g

oven-cooked chicken

crunchy drumsticks

ingredients

1 kg (2 lb) chicken drumsticks
2 tablespoons curry paste
60 g (2 oz) vinegar-flavored corn chips
  or potato crisps
boiled rice or salad
mild chutney to serve
serves 4

i

preparation time
5 minutes

cooking time
40 minutes

**nutritional value
per serve**
fat: 8.5 g
carbohydrate: 2.9 g
protein: 17.1 g

1 Preheat oven to 180°C (350°F, gas mark 4). Rinse drumsticks and pat dry. With fingers rub the curry paste well into the skin of the drumsticks. Crush the corn chips or potato crisps and press onto the drumsticks.

2 Place on a rack over a shallow baking pan. Bake in a preheated oven for 35–40 minutes. Serve hot with boiled rice and a portion of chutney on the side. They may also be served cold with salad.

easy apricot and mango chicken loaf

ingredients

700 g (1 lb 7 oz) ground chicken
60 g (2 oz) fresh breadcrumbs
90 g (3 oz) green onions,
   chopped including green part
1 tablespoon finely chopped parsley
2 tablespoons diced dried apricots
1 tablespoon mango chutney
1 egg
1 teaspoon salt
$^1/_4$ teaspoon pepper
oil for greasing
serves 6

1 Preheat oven to 180°C (350°F, gas mark 4). In a large bowl, place chicken mince. Add breadcrumbs, green onions, parsley, apricots, chutney, egg, salt and pepper. With your hand, mix and knead mixture for 2–3 minutes to combine ingredients well and to give a fine texture.

2 Grease an 8.5 x 3 x 2 inch loaf tin with oil. Place in the chicken mixture. Place in oven and bake for 50–55 minutes. To test insert skewer into center and if clear juice appears it is cooked. If juice is a pink color further cooking is required. Rest in the tin 10 minutes before turning out.

i

preparation time
8 minutes

cooking time
55 minutes,
plus 10 minutes
standing

**nutritional value
per serve**
fat: 7.7 g
carbohydrate: 6.6 g
protein: 15.7 g

apricot-glazed chicken with savory stuffing

ingredients

1.5 kg (3 lb) fresh chicken
½ lemon

apricot glaze
160 g (5½ oz) apricot jam
1 tablespoon soy sauce
1 tablespoon lemon juice
2 tablespoons white vinegar
1 tablespoon water

easy stuffing
3-4 slices bacon, chopped
1 large onion, finely chopped
1 ¾ cups (350 g, 11½ oz) long-grain rice, rinsed
3 cups (750 ml, 24 fl oz) boiling water
2 teaspoons apricot glaze
2 teaspoons soy sauce
2 teaspoons mixed dried herbs
2 tablespoons chopped parsley
1 tablespoon flour, for gravy

serves 4

i

preparation time
20 minutes

cooking time
1½ hours

nutritional value
per serve
fat: 5.8 g
carbohydrate: 16.9 g
protein: 13.9 g

1 Preheat oven to 180°C (350°F, gas mark 5). Rinse out the chicken cavity, pat dry with paper towel and place the lemon half in the cavity. Tie drumsticks ends together with kitchen string or truss. In a saucepan, combine the apricot jam, soy sauce, lemon juice, vinegar and water and heat gently while stirring. Brush the chicken all over with glaze.

2 Place on an adjustable rack, breast-side down. Add a cup of water to the dish and place in the preheated oven for 40 minutes. Brush again with glaze and turn breast-side up, brush with glaze and continue to cook for 40–50 minutes more, until cooked when tested.

3 When chicken is placed in the oven, prepare the stuffing. Place all ingredients in a lidded casserole dish and place on a shelf in the oven under the chicken. Cook for 40 minutes then remove from oven and stand covered for 10 minutes.

4 When chicken is cooked, remove from dish and cover with foil to rest. Skim fat from roasting pan and add about 1 cup (250 ml, 8 fl oz) water to dissolve any cooked-on pan juices. Pour into a small saucepan. Add 1 tablespoon flour blended with a little water and stir until it thickens and boils. Carve chicken and serve with rice stuffing, gravy and vegetable accompaniments.

tandoori chicken

Ingredients

2 (each about 1 kg, 2 lb) small chickens
3 tablespoons tandoori curry paste
200 g (7 oz) natural yogurt
2 tablespoons lemon juice
2 tablespoons melted butter
$^1/_2$ cup (125 ml, 4 fl oz) water
lettuce for garnish
1 onion, cut into rings for garnish
1 tomato, cut into wedges for garnish
serves 4–6

1 Rinse chickens and pat dry. Make deep gashes in the thighs, drumsticks and breast with a sharp knife. Mix the tandoori curry paste, yogurt, lemon juice and melted butter together.

2 In a large non-metallic dish, place chickens. Spread curry mixture all over the chickens, rubbing well into the gashes. Cover and refrigerate for 12 hours or more.

3 Preheat oven to 190°C (370°F, gas mark 5). Place chickens on a roasting rack in a baking dish, spoon over any of the remaining marinade. Add water to the base of the dish to prevent charring of pan juices.

4 Place chickens in the oven and cook for 1 hour. Baste with pan juices during cooking. Stand covered with foil 10 minutes before serving. Cut chickens into serving portions and place on platter lined with lettuce leaves. Garnish with onion rings and tomato.

preparation time
15 minutes,
plus 12 hours
marinating

cooking time
1 hour

nutritional value
fat: 11.6 g
carbohydrate: 0.7 g
protein: 16.5 g

roasted herb chicken with pears

ingredients

juice of 2 lemons
salt and black pepper
12 chicken drumsticks, skinned
6 firm pears, peeled, halved, cored and
 cut crossways into quarter-inch slices
150 ml (5 fl oz) white wine
1 tablespoon chopped fresh thyme
1 tablespoon chopped fresh tarragon
1 tablespoon chopped fresh rosemary
serves 6

i

preparation time
15 minutes, plus
30 minutes
marinating and
10 minutes
resting

cooking time
1 hour 10 minutes

**nutritional value
per serve**
fat: 3.8 g
carbohydrate: 4.9 g
protein: 11.2 g

1 In a bowl, mix together the lemon juice, salt and pepper. Put the chicken into a shallow, non-metallic bowl. Pour over the lemon juice, salt and pepper and rub into the skin with your fingertips. Cover and marinate in the refrigerator for 30 minutes.

2 Preheat the oven to 200°C (400°F, gas mark 6). Arrange the pears in a deep ovenproof dish, then top with the chicken and pour over the marinating juices. Pour over the wine and sprinkle with the thyme, tarragon and rosemary. Cover the dish with foil.

3 Cook for 1 hour, basting once or twice, until the chicken is tender. Remove the foil and increase the oven temperature to 230°C (450°F, gas mark 8). Cook for a further 10 minutes or until the chicken is cooked through and the skin has browned. Leave it to rest, covered, for 10 minutes before serving.

roasted herb stuffed chicken

ingredients

4 chicken breasts, on the bone with
   skin on

herb stuffing

2 tablespoons thick natural yogurt
1 clove garlic, minced
1 teaspoon olive oil
2 tablespoons finely chopped mint
2 tablespoons finely chopped flat-leaf
   parsley
2 tablespoons finely chopped oregano
2 tablespoons finely chopped thyme
2 tablespoons finely chopped dill
2 green onions, finely chopped
salt and finely ground black pepper

serves 4-6

1 In a small bowl, combine together all the herb stuffing ingredients and mix well.

2 Using your finger tips, scoop up a quarter of the mixture and gently push under the skin of the chicken. Run your fingers over the skin to smooth the stuffing out. Attach skin with a toothpick to side of breast if needed. Repeat with the remaining pieces. Cover, and refrigerate for 1½ hours.

3 Pre-heat the oven to 180°C (350°F, gas mark 4). Place the chicken on a roasting rack and cook in the oven for 15–20 minutes.

4 Remove to a chopping board. Remove bone carefully and cut into thick diagonal slices. Skim fat from pan juices and pour over the chicken.

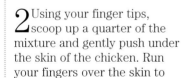

preparation time
15 minutes,
plus 1½ hours
refrigeration

cooking time
20 minutes

**nutritional value
per serve**
fat: 9.9 g
carbohydrate: 0.3 g
protein: 18.7 g

roast chicken with basil and red onion

ingredients

1.5 kg (3 lb) chicken
1 handful fresh basil leaves
120 ml (4 fl oz) extra virgin olive oil
juice of $\frac{1}{2}$ lemon
sea salt and freshly ground black pepper
4 medium red onions
zest of $\frac{1}{2}$ lemon, grated
1 garlic clove, minced

serves 4

i

preparation time
20 minutes,
plus 10 minutes
resting

cooking time
1 hour 10 minutes

nutritional value per serve
fat: 13.3 g
carbohydrate: 1.2 g
protein: 14.2 g

1 Preheat the oven to 190°C (375°F, gas mark 5). Place the chicken in a roasting pan. Gently work the skin away from the flesh with your fingers and tuck about 6–7 basil leaves under the breast skin. Place the remaining basil in a blender with the olive oil, lemon juice and seasoning and blend until smooth. Brush the chicken with half the basil oil. Place in preheated oven and roast for 40 minutes.

2 Peel the onion and slice off the root end to give a flat base. Make four cuts, in a criss-cross shape, across the top of each onion to come only halfway down, so the onions open slightly. Combine the lemon zest with the garlic and sprinkle over the onions.

3 Add the onions to the chicken in the pan and brush well with some of the basil oil. Brush the remaining oil over the chicken and cook for a further 40 minutes or until cooked through. Cover and allow the chicken to rest for 10 minutes before carving.

oven-baked parmesan chicken

ingredients

60 g (2 oz) fresh breadcrumbs, made
   from country-style bread
75 g (3 oz) parmesan, finely grated
2 green onions, finely chopped
finely grated zest and juice of
   $\frac{1}{2}$ lemon
4 tablespoons butter, melted
sea salt and freshly ground black pepper
4 chicken breast fillets
2 tablespoons chopped fresh parsley
serves 4

preparation time
15 minutes

cooking time
20 minutes

**nutritional value
per serve**
fat: 9.9 g
carbohydrate: 2.6 g
protein: 20 g

1 Preheat the oven to 190°C (375°F, gas mark 5). In a small bowl, mix together the breadcrumbs, parmesan, green onions, lemon zest, butter, salt and pepper.

2 Divide the mixture between the chicken breasts and using a fork, press the mixture on top, to form an even coat.

3 Transfer the chicken breasts to a greased shallow oven dish and bake for 20 minutes. Remove the chicken and keep warm. Add the lemon juice and parsley to the buttery juices in the dish and mix well. Pour these juices over the chicken and serve immediately.

chicken and leek flan with almond topping

ingredients

2 frozen savory 20 cm flan cases
1 tablespoon canola oil
2 leeks, trimmed, washed and thinly
  sliced
500 g (1 lb) chicken breast fillets, sliced
  into quarter-inch slices
200 g (7 oz) button mushrooms, sliced
1 tablespoon lemon juice
1 cup (250 ml, 8 fl oz) water
1 cup (250 ml, 8 fl oz) milk
45 g (1¹/₂ oz) packet cream of chicken
  soup mix
2 eggs, lightly beaten
¹/₄ teaspoon nutmeg
100 g (3¹/₂ oz) flaked almonds
serves 4–6 per flan

1 Preheat oven to 180°C (350°F, gas mark 4). Place the frozen flan cases on a tray in the oven and blind bake for 10–15 minutes as directed. Remove and set aside.

2 Heat oil in a large saucepan and cook leeks for 5 minutes until soft. Remove to a bowl. Add the chicken pieces to saucepan and cook for 1 minute on each side. Add mushrooms and lemon juice, turn down heat and simmer for 3 minutes. Return the leeks to the saucepan and set aside.

3 In a saucepan, combine water and milk and stir in the soup mix. Place over heat and bring to the boil while stirring. Cook until thick. Pour into the chicken mixture and stir to combine. Allow the mixture to cool a little before stirring in the eggs and nutmeg.

4 Remove the blind bake from the flan cases and fill with the chicken filling. Sprinkle each with the flaked almonds to make a dense covering. Bake in the pre-heated oven for 25–30 minutes until filling is set.

preparation time
15 minutes

cooking time
35 minutes

nutritional value
fat: 8.7 g
carbohydrate: 4.6 g
protein: 11.9 g

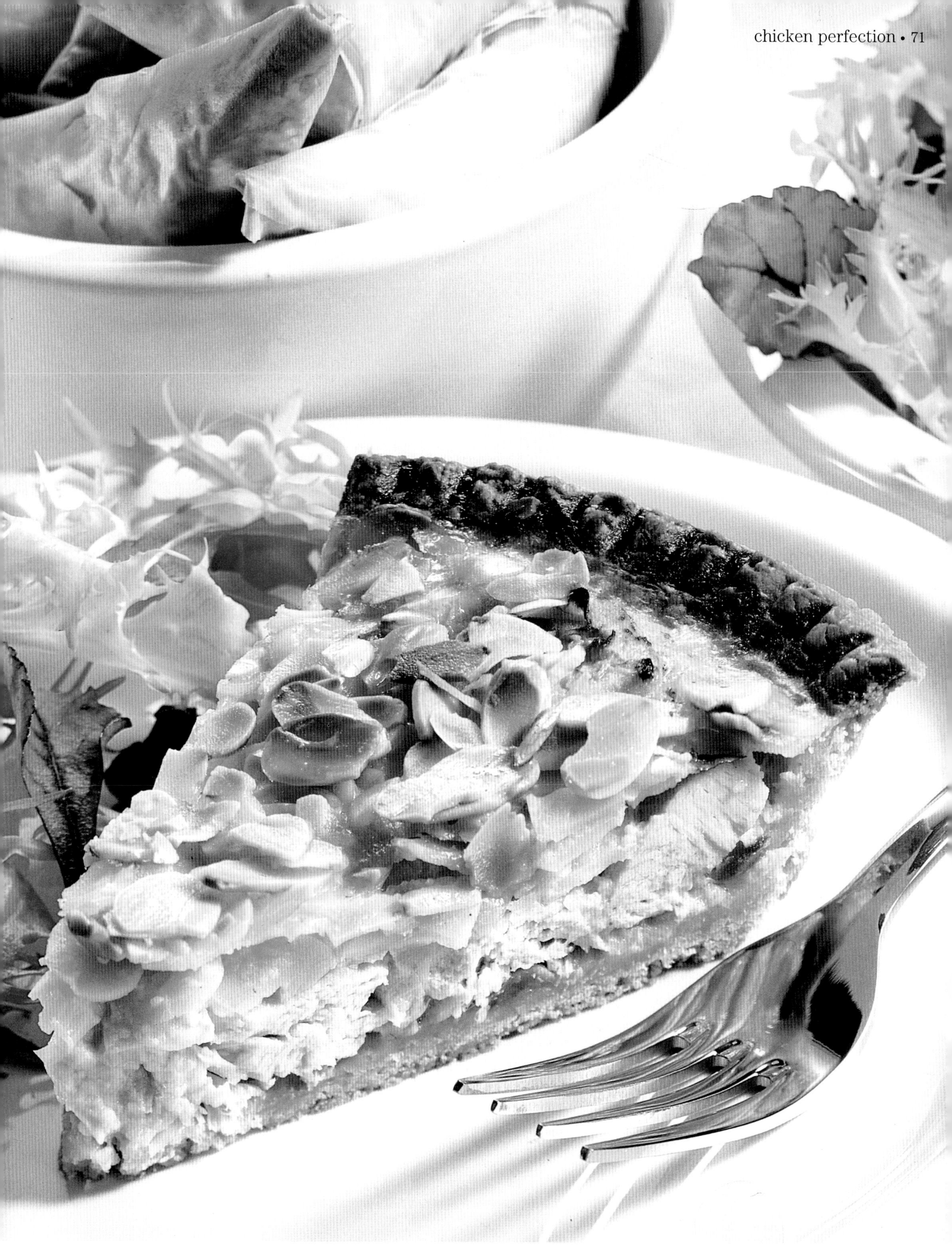

chicken with ricotta, rocket and roasted red bell pepper

ingredients

220 g (7½ oz) fresh ricotta
1 bunch rocket, roughly chopped
45 g (1½ oz) pine nuts, toasted
½ red bell pepper, roasted and
    finely chopped
salt and freshly ground pepper
4 (each about 185–220 g, 6-7 oz)
    chicken breasts, on bone with skin on
1 tablespoon butter
1 cup (250 ml, 8 fl oz) chicken stock

serves 4

1 Preheat the oven to 200°C (400°F, gas mark 6). In a small bowl, combine ricotta, rocket, pine nuts, bell pepper, pepper and salt. Mix together until smooth.

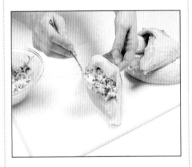

2 Place 1–2 tablespoons of ricotta mixture under the skin of each chicken breast. Lightly grease a baking dish.

3 In the dish, place chicken breasts and sprinkle with salt and pepper. Place 1 teaspoon butter on each breast. Pour stock around the chicken and bake for 20–25 minutes. The bone may be carefully removed before serving. Serve chicken with pan-juices.

i

preparation time
20 minutes

cooking time
25 minutes

nutritional value per serve
fat: 10 g
carbohydrate: 0.6 g
protein: 14.7 g

chicken breasts with mushrooms and cream

ingredients

2 tablespoons butter
1 clove garlic, minced
125 g (4 oz) chestnut mushrooms, finely chopped
125 g (4 oz) chestnut mushrooms, sliced
salt and black pepper
1 tablespoon chopped fresh flat-leaf parsley
1 tablespoon chopped fresh tarragon
4 large chicken breast fillets
150 ml (5 fl oz) chicken stock
150 ml (5 fl oz) sparkling or dry white wine
150 ml (5 fl oz) heavy cream
fresh flat-leaf parsley to garnish
serves 4

preparation time
20 minutes, plus 10 minutes cooling

cooking time
45 minutes

nutritional value per serve
fat: 6.8 g
carbohydrate: 0.4 g
protein: 15.3 g

1 Melt half the butter in a skillet. Add the garlic and chopped mushrooms, reserving the sliced mushrooms. Add salt and pepper and cook, stirring, over a high heat for 5 minutes or until softened. Place into a bowl, stir in the parsley and tarragon and leave to cool for 10 minutes.

2 Make a slit down the center of each chicken breast, then insert the tip of a knife into either side of the slit to open it out into a pocket. Place the chicken in a baking dish and spoon the mushroom mixture into the pockets.

3 Preheat the oven to 180°C (350°F, gas mark 4). Melt the remaining butter in a skillet.

Add the sliced mushrooms, salt and pepper and cook over a high heat for 3 minutes. Add the stock, wine and cream and bring to the boil. Simmer for 10 minutes or until thickened slightly. Pour over the chicken, cover with foil and cook for 20–25 minutes, basting halfway through. To serve, spoon the sauce over the chicken and garnish with parsley.

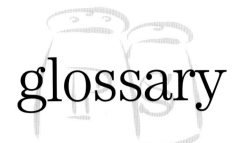

glossary

al dente: Italian term to describe pasta and rice that are cooked until tender but still firm to the bite.

bake blind: to bake pastry cases without their fillings. Line the raw pastry case with wax paper and fill with raw rice or dried beans to prevent collapsed sides and puffed base. Remove paper and fill 5 minutes before completion of cooking time.

baste: to spoon hot cooking liquid over food at intervals during cooking to moisten and flavor it.

beat: to make a mixture smooth with rapid and regular motions using a spatula, wire whisk or electric mixer; to make a mixture light and smooth by enclosing air.

beurre manié: equal quantities of butter and flour mixed together to a smooth paste and stirred little by little into a soup, stew or sauce while on the heat to thicken. Stop adding when desired thickness results.

bind: to add egg or a thick sauce to hold ingredients together when cooked.

blanch: to plunge some foods into boiling water for less than a minute and immediately plunge into iced water. This is to brighten the color of some vegetables; to remove skin from tomatoes and nuts.

blend: to mix 2 or more ingredients thoroughly together; do not confuse with blending in an electric blender.

boil: to cook in a liquid brought to boiling point and kept there.

boiling point: when bubbles rise continually and break over the entire surface of the liquid, reaching a temperature of 100°C (212°F). In some cases food is held at this high temperature for a few seconds then heat is turned to low for slower cooking. See simmer.

bouquet garni: a bundle of several herbs tied together with string for easy removal, placed into pots of stock, soups and stews for flavor. A few sprigs of fresh thyme, parsley and bay leaf are used. Can be purchased in sachet form for convenience.

caramelize: to heat sugar in a heavy pan until it liquefies and develops a caramel color. Vegetables such as blanched carrots and sautéed onions may be sprinkled with sugar and caramelized.

chill: to place in the refrigerator or stir over ice until cold.

clarify: to make a liquid clear by removing sediments and impurities. To melt fat and remove any sediment.

coat: to dust or roll food items in flour to cover the surface before the food is cooked. Also, to coat in flour, egg and breadcrumbs.

cool: to stand at room temperature until some or all heat is removed, e.g., cool a little, cool completely.

cream: to make creamy and fluffy by working the mixture with the back of a wooden spoon, usually refers to creaming butter and sugar or margarine. May also be creamed with an electric mixer.

croutons: small cubes of bread, toasted or fried, used as an addition to salads or as a garnish to soups and stews.

crudite: raw vegetable sticks served with a dipping sauce.

crumb: to coat foods in flour, egg and breadcrumbs to form a protective coating for foods that are fried. Also adds flavor, texture and enhances appearance.

cube: to cut into small pieces with six even sides, e.g., cubes of meat.

cut in: to combine fat and flour using 2 knives scissor fashion or with a pastry blender, to make pastry.

deglaze: to dissolve dried out cooking juices left on the bottom and sides of a roasting dish or skillet. Add a little water, wine or stock, scrape and stir over heat until dissolved. Resulting liquid is used to make a flavorsome gravy or added to a sauce or casserole.

degrease: to skim fat from the surface of cooking liquids, e.g., stocks, soups, casseroles.

dice: to cut into small cubes.

dredge: to heavily coat with powdered sugar, sugar, flour or cornstarch.

dressing: a mixture added to completed dishes to add moisture and flavor, e.g., salads, cooked vegetables.

drizzle: to pour in a fine thread-like stream moving over a surface.

egg wash: beaten egg with milk or water used to brush over pastry, bread dough or cookies to give a sheen and golden brown color.

essence: a strong flavoring liquid, usually made by distillation. Only a few drops are needed to flavor.

fillet: a piece of prime meat, fish or poultry that is boneless or has all bones removed.

flake: to separate cooked fish into flakes, removing any bones and skin, using 2 forks.

flame: to ignite warmed alcohol over food or to pour into a pan with food, ignite then serve.

flute: to make decorative indentations around the pastry edge before baking.

fold in: combining of a light, whipped or creamed mixture with other ingredients. Add a portion of the other ingredients at a time and mix using a gentle circular motion, over and under the mixture so that air will not be lost. Use a silver spoon or spatula.

glaze: to brush or coat food with a liquid that will give the finished product a glossy appearance, and on baked products, a golden brown color.

grease: to rub the surface of a metal or heatproof dish with oil or fat, to prevent the food from sticking.

herbed butter: softened butter mixed with finely chopped fresh herbs and re-chilled. Used to serve on grilled meats and fish.

hors d'ouvre: small savory foods served as an appetizer, popularly known today as "finger food".

infuse: to steep foods in a liquid until the liquid absorbs their flavor.

joint: to cut poultry and game into serving pieces by dividing at the joint.

julienne: to cut some food, e.g., vegetables and processed meats into fine strips the length of matchsticks. Used for inclusion in salads or as a garnish to cooked dishes.

knead: to work a yeast dough in a pressing, stretching and folding motion with the heel of the hand until smooth and elastic to develop the gluten strands. Non-yeast doughs should be lightly and quickly handled as gluten development is not desired.

line: to cover the inside of a baking pan with paper for the easy removal of the cooked product from the baking pan.

macerate: to stand fruit in a syrup, liqueur or spirit to give added flavor.

marinade: a flavored liquid, into which food is placed for some time to give it flavor and to tenderize. Marinades include an acid ingredient such as vinegar or wine, oil and seasonings.

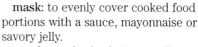

mask: to evenly cover cooked food portions with a sauce, mayonnaise or savory jelly.

pan-fry: to fry foods in a small amount of fat or oil, sufficient to coat the bottom of the pan.

parboil: to boil until partially cooked. The food is then finished by some other method.

pare: to peel the skin from vegetables and fruit. Peel is the popular term but pare is the name given to the knife used; paring knife.

pith: the white lining between the rind and flesh of oranges, grapefruit and lemons.

pit: to remove stones or seeds from olives, cherries, dates.

pitted: the olives, cherries, dates, etc., with the stone removed, e.g., purchase pitted dates.

poach: to simmer gently in enough hot liquid to almost cover the food so shape will be retained.

pound: to flatten meats with a meat mallet; to reduce to a paste or small particles with a mortar and pestle.

simmer: to cook in liquid just below boiling point at about 96°C (205°F) with small bubbles rising gently to the surface.

skim: to remove fat or froth from the surface of simmering food.

stock: the liquid produced when meat, poultry, fish or vegetables have been simmered in water to extract the flavor. Used as a base for soups, sauces, casseroles, etc. Convenience stock products are available.

sweat: to cook sliced onions or vegetables, in a small amount of butter in a covered pan over low heat, to soften them and release flavor without coloring.

conversions

measurements differ from country to country, so it's important to understand what the differences are. This Measurements Guide gives you simple "at-a-glance" information for using the recipes in this book, wherever you may be.

Cooking is not an exact science – minor variations in measurements won't make a difference to your cooking.

equipment

There is a difference in the size of measuring cups used internationally, but the difference is minimal (only 2–3 teaspoons). We use the Australian standard metric measurements in our recipes:

1 teaspoon ....5 ml   1 tablespoon....20 ml
1/2 cup......125 ml   1 cup.....250 ml
4 cups...1 liter

Measuring cups come in sets of one cup (250 ml), 1/2 cup (125 ml), 1/3 cup (80 ml) and 1/4 cup (60 ml). Use these for measuring liquids and certain dry ingredients.
Measuring spoons come in a set of four and should be used for measuring dry and liquid ingredients.
When using cup or spoon measures always make them level (unless the recipe indicates otherwise).

dry versus wet ingredients

While this system of measures is consistent for liquids, it's more difficult to quantify dry ingredients. For instance, one level cup equals: 200 g of brown sugar; 210 g of superfine sugar; and 110 g of powdered sugar.

When measuring dry ingredients such as flour, don't push the flour down or shake it into the cup. It is best just to spoon the flour in until it reaches the desired amount. When measuring liquids use a clear vessel indicating metric levels.

Always use medium eggs (1.5-2.5 oz) when eggs are required in a recipe.

dry

metric (grams)	imperial (ounces)
30 g	1 oz
60 g	2 oz
90 g	3 oz
100 g	3 1/2 oz
125 g	4 oz
150 g	5 oz
185 g	6 oz
200 g	7 oz
250 g	8 oz
280 g	9 oz
315 g	10 oz
330 g	11 oz
370 g	12 oz
400 g	13 oz
440 g	14 oz
470 g	15 oz
500 g	16 oz (1 lb)
750 g	24 oz (1 1/2 lb)
1000 g (1 kg)	32 oz (2 lb)

liquids

metric (milliliters)	imperial (fluid ounces)
30 ml	1 fl oz
60 ml	2 fl oz
90 ml	3 fl oz
100 ml	3 1/2 fl oz
125 ml	4 fl oz
150 ml	5 fl oz
190 ml	6 fl oz
250 ml	8 fl oz
300 ml	10 fl oz
500 ml	16 fl oz
600 ml	20 fl oz (1 pint)*
1000 ml (1 liter)	32 fl oz

*Note: an American pint is 16 fl oz.

oven
Your oven should always be at the right temperature before placing the food in it to be cooked. Note that if your oven doesn't have a fan you may need to cook food for a little longer.

microwave
It is difficult to give an exact cooking time for microwave cooking. It is best to watch what you are cooking closely to monitor its progress.

standing time
Many foods continue to cook when you take them out of the oven or microwave. If a recipe states that the food needs to "stand" after cooking, be sure not to overcook the dish.

can sizes
The can sizes available in your supermarket or grocery store may not be the same as specified in the recipe. Don't worry if there is a small variation in size—it's unlikely to make a difference to the end result.

cooking temperatures	ºC (celsius)	ºF (fahrenheit)	gas mark
very slow	120	250	1/2
slow	150	300	2
moderately slow	160	315	2-3
moderate	180	350	4
moderate hot	190	375	5
	200	400	6
hot	220	425	7
very hot	230	450	8
	240	475	9
	250	500	10

index